the wisdom i can't teach

PAUL COYNE

The Wisdom I Can't Teach © 2025 by Paul Coyne

All rights reserved.

No part of this book may be reproduced, distributed, or transmitted in any form or by any means, including photocopying, recording, or other electronic or mechanical methods, or by any information storage and retrieval system, without the prior written permission of the author, except as permitted by U.S. copyright law. For permission requests, contact Paul Coyne.

Each of these poems has been inspired from numerous events over the lifetime of the author and are not referencing any specific events or individuals.

print ISBN: 979-8-35098-700-3
ebook ISBN: 979-8-35098-701-0

Printed in the United States of America

For Thomas

CONTENTS

The Wisdom I Can't Teach 1
Destination: Greatness 2
Creation 5
Bound 6
A Baby Is Crying 7
Choose 8
The Rules 9
The Force 10
Who, What, Where, When, Why? 11
The Beacon and the Candle 12
Once In a While 13
The Value of a Coin 14
The Tide 15
The Forest 16
When It Stops 18
The Farm 19
Know and Protect 20
The Dungeon 21
The Precipice 22
Nothing 23
The Quest 24
Buried 25
The Father 26
Out of Line 27
Bending Reality 28
Weak and Strong 29
Here and Now 30
Who Will I Become? 31
Someone I Wish to Meet 32
What Have I Done? 33
The Ladder 34
The Book of Love 36

The Carousel 37
Sheep 38
Boundless Choices 39
The Other Beasts 40
The Blind 41
Fed 42
Why Don't I 43
The Ditch 44
Home 45
Perfection 46
The Long Game 47
A Higher Plane 48
Lost and Found 50
Leaves 51
Did You Run There Wanting More? 52
Lonely 53
The Face at the Gates 54
The Gift of Today 56
My Heart Has Known the Darkness 57
Congratulations 58
Fight or Flight 59
The It Factor 60
On an Island Out at Sea 61
The Table 62
How Are You? 63
Watch 64
Memories and Dreams 65
The Lighthouse 66
The Bell 67
Beehive 68
Applause 69
Confidence and Competence 70
Who Are We? 71
The Person Is Us 72

Are We The Same? 74
The Snake in the Grass 75
The Mistake 76
Pier 77
The Treasure 78
The Mirror Maze 79
A Thousand Rooms 80
How To Respond to a Sincere "Thank You" 81
Requirements for Every Human Interaction 82
Vision 83
Us Vs. Them 84
The Embers 85
Why Am I Here? 86
Power 87
I Am the Clock 88
Ace In the Hole 89
Planet Me 90
A Chance Encounter 92
Chain of Hearts 93
The Holidays 94
The Man Who Tells 95
Greatness Never Dies 96
Crows 97
The King and The Jester 98
I am 99
The Churn 100
Speak and Be Heard 101
Vampire in Reverse 102
I Can Save Them 104
The Stadium 105
Where Have They Gone? 106
Where Do I Hide? 108
If The World Will Talk About Me 109
The Horizon 110

The Wisdom I Can't Teach

The wisdom I can't teach
But I must teach it

The peak I cannot reach
But I must reach it

The answer I can't find
And I'm running out of time

The only mine that can be mined
Is the mind that already is mine

The wisdom I can unleash
And if I teach the treasure

The peak we then reach together
Is a height we can't measure

Destination: Greatness

I heard the whistle blowing
I saw the chimney steam
I smelled the burning fire
Inside I knew my dream

I thought I had to find it
I thought I was too late
I thought I was behind it
I thought this was my fate

Then I arrived and saw the sign
I read the information
Destination: Greatness
It hadn't left the station

The first-class car was out of reach
The middle car reduced
All the seats were taken
So, I stood in the caboose

This was that which I was promised
This was that which I was told
Lucky to be there on the train
All along we rolled

No one else could see the same
Out my window from the back
But on the path behind us
Someone had switched the track

It was still slow enough for me to jump
But because I felt I should
I started walking toward the front
To warn everyone I could

THE WISDOM I CAN'T TEACH

I said, "Please, I beg you listen
This journey must curtail
The train was supposed to lead to greatness
And now it's destined to derail"

Most ignored my plea to save them
Some tried to silence and deprive
Up front they said if you know that much
Then we should let you drive

I didn't know how to drive a train
I thought sometimes I couldn't
But I knew where we should be headed
And where I knew we shouldn't

I called the operator down the line
I said, "Please make the switch
The people wanted greatness
But they don't know which track is which"

Some didn't notice we had changed
Some voiced their strong objection
Some were glad that we were back on course
Some were mad we changed direction

But either way we found it
Either way it's not too late
For no one will be left behind
When fulfillment is our fate

We will add more cars for everyone
We will make more seats as well
Still tireless in my quest to help
"All aboard!" I yell

PAUL COYNE

To let you off or let you on
I won't stop but I will slow
Destination: Greatness
Do you want to go?

Hear the whistle blowing,
See the chimney steam,
Feel the burning fire
All aboard — and find your dream

Creation

Take two who know that there
Is more to life than just what is in reach.
Not too much of either.
Yet not less than each.

Tick tock until
Eventually the stings of life
Abated. Love
Culminates
Until they know
Perfection is created.

Bound

Bound within each being, is a soul beneath the soil
Begging back to break the bonds of nature's mortal coil

Some souls succumb to saying, that their world is theirs to build
And fill their life with what they wish, still deeply unfulfilled

Others toil and labor, accepting daily their deflation
For each day brings them closer, to finding true salvation

They are bound to be united, bound to be at home
But longing for this moment, these souls, too, begin to roam

Be still and hear Him calling, be still and know today
Be still and fear no longer, be still and hear Him say,

"You are not truly bound within, nor are you truly bound to be
The battle has been won, my child, you are already free"

A Baby Is Crying

A baby is crying
Think now what to do
Is he hungry or tired?
Does he need love from you?

But he needs not a thing
That's not why he cries
He's come here to save
From the sin and the lies

He cries so you notice
He cries so you know
He hopes that you love Him
But He won't make it so

It is you who are tired
And in need to be nourished
It is you trying so hard
For the answer to flourish

All He asks is you sit there
And let Him do the rest
If you want to stop crying
Then you must tell Him yes

The manger is open
The heavens are too
His heart is the answer
He's come just for you

Choose

You may feel it coming
Or be completely unaware
You may be at the ready
Or have no time to prepare

You may try to run away
Or even run right toward
You may act like you are mesmerized
Or act like you are bored

You may try to fight it
Or you might embrace
You may stand tall and meet it
Or hide your timid face

Love may be life's limerick
Or it could be death in prose
Funny you can act the same
No matter which you chose

The Rules

If you rise up from your seat
And they tell you sit right there
Take the load off from your feet
You can stand up from your chair

If you start to use your voice,
And speaking means defiance
Do not howl, quietly rejoice
You'll be heard most from your silence

If they tell you look don't touch
When your hands will start to spread
The little lost will gain very much
When you reach out your heart instead

The game of life is yours to win
You must abide by all the rules
But if you live confined within,
Count yourself among the fools

For most will live within the lines
Until time will not allow
Stand and speak and seek to love
And know your time is now

The Force

Consuming that which stands opposed
Scorching all within its sphere
Blazing through the barriers
What does the fire fear?

Pulling all back to itself
Making impact in a hurry
Crashing down upon the stone
Why would the great wave worry?

Rising up alone above all else
Blinding those who look straight on
Squelching what once did surround
Where's the doubt within the dawn?

You are the fire, the wave, the dawn
Do not fear or doubt or hide
For the greatest force of nature
Is the one that dwells inside

Who, What, Where, When, Why?

Who are the selfish
If there are none giving?
Who are the dead
If there are none living?

What is the wrong
If there is no right?
What is the dark
If there is no light?

Where is the sky
If there is no ground?
Where is the lost
If there is no found?

When is the peak
If there is no climb?
When is it late
If there is no time?

Why would we cry
If there was nothing to feel?
Why would we dream
If nothing was real?

The Beacon and the Candle

Not dimmer nor a glimmer
In the abyss the same they stay
Without a light in sight
There is not a thing to take away

Yet, while those who live in darkness
Are trapped inside the night
If they find the beacon
They recognize the light

But those blinded by the brightness
They will wish they knew
For they won't see around them
Until the light goes out of view

Know the light and know the darkness
There is nothing you can't handle
Don't fly any closer to the sun
Don't forget you have a candle

Once In a While

For a while it may seem
Like your whole life is on trial
Your smile fades and you become
Buried beneath the pile

For a while it will feel
Like you are stranded on the isle
You're exile now, not just from others
But to yourself, there is a mile

For a while you will think
You should just give up but don't
Just remember when it hurts
Once in a while it won't

PAUL COYNE

The Value of a Coin

Do I feel good?
Do I feel bad?
Am I happy?
Am I sad?

The secret to fulfillment
Is to make them join
They are both two sides
Of the exact same coin

When the bud of gloom appears,
Don't reach to try to nip it
Let it bloom there next to joy
It's on the other side, flip it

The emotions are different
But you'll find it never fails
To forget which side is heads
To not know which side is tails

Try to move toward the front
And remember the back
But if you can't see either
And the coins are cracked

Know that viewed from any angle
Or even when it's not in view
The coin always holds its value
Just the same as you

The Tide

When the ocean is high
Nothing stops tidal powers
Yet the shore will be dry
Within a few hours

At low tide of the sea
The beach can only get wetter
If it's as bad as can be
It can only get better

The greatest struggles are sweeter
When you start to get stronger
The whole point of life
Could just be those parts, but longer

PAUL COYNE

The Forest

Amidst the barren desert
After the great storm caused all to flee
Towering to the sky alone
Remained just one last tree

Firm and deeply rooted
Tall and straight without careen
The purest stood when all else fell
Just one redwood evergreen

Season after season
In isolation was its toil
Then to the left of this tall tree
Became some fertile soil

Every branch and every leaf
Dripped their last drops below
And though the land was fertile
The soil did not grow

Mighty yet forsaken
In the dark and desert night
The tree was out of water when
Something sprouted from the right

The tree had given all it had
Water it could give no more
It simply did what trees must do
The roots extended from its core

Far beneath the desert sand
The tree gave all just out of view
The second tree grew just as tall
Until its roots extended too

Behold the million redwoods
Each independent tree stands tall
Trace the roots and you will find
The reason for them all

So grow and grow much taller
And find your place in chorus
One tree stood very tall alone
So you would have a forest

When It Stops

Listen close and hear the sounds
Of the bedraggled and the broken
The echoes of the truth remain
Though the word was never spoken

Beating on yet blinded
When it stops is not a thought
For even when it's close
It seems to stop but it does not

Stopping yet not ceasing
Is how they live because
They do not know what happens
When it stops, until it does

The Farm

Plant the seeds and till and tend
Then reap just what you sow
Marvel at the handsome harvest
Higher does it grow

Stay calm in the calamity
The crops are cut without alarm
The secret to prosperity
Is never bet the farm

Sell the produce from the field
And the livestock in the pen
They are not what is most valued
You can do it all again

First you think you're growing crops
Then you think the business too
They both grow faster if you realize
You are only growing you

Know and Protect

Ten rejoiced and then proclaimed
How they saw and believed
One that did not see himself
Made not to be deceived
And then the one who doubted, now on par with other men
Saw with both his eyes and heart, more than the other ten

Ever innately joyous
Dance in riches that abound
Worry not of sorrow
As the fortune has been found
Revel in the rapture, and yet take time to reflect
Decide, in order to sustain, to guard and to protect

The Dungeon

To stay inside the dungeon of the dark
Remains the greatest travesty of all
The candle flickers but can find no spark

To hide within the ever-growing wall
Will lead the heart to long and to beseech
No one can hear the whisper of the call

The promised key remains just out of reach
Inside afflicted torment starts to grow
No thought can find the meaning of the speech

So sad it is to stay and not to go
Inside the darkness trapped for ever more
To ask and never find the answer though

Where does the light perpetually pour?
The other side of a wide-open door

The Precipice

We plan the charted course and we begin
To walk until the boundless lanes compress.
We lose everywhere that we used to win.
In every direction we seek to spin.
We move rapidly but do not progress.

It forces us to pause and promptly stall.
The danger starting to draw near and loom
With all paths leading to the stormy squall.
The precipice lies at the edge of all.
At the end of each there is our doom.

Our future now reduced to a great lie
As all roads lead to a destructive end.
Then we wonder if we should even try.
But we are not meant just to walk but fly
And cannot exist unless we transcend.

Nothing

Nothing to teach if there is no class
Nothing to catch if there is no pass

Nothing to judge if not for the jury
Nothing to fight if not for foe's fury

No villain in sight if there is no hero
No counting the one if there is no zero

What is a sister, if there is no brother?
Who are we all without one another?

The Quest

Whether we fall or we rise
Life keeps on progressing
Each fall is a gift
Each gift is a blessing

For it appears that we fell
But it was only a stumble
Then appears we did well
Yet we must stay humble

If you reach the goal
You may become better
But the best will be trapped
And confined in a fetter

For it is not just each end
But indeed a life's quest
That will make the better
Turn into the best

Buried

Buried in the love received
There's no doubt of what is pure
Buried here in this disease
Is the way to find the cure
Buried in our bodies
Is the soul that we neglect
Buried in our minds
We find all that we forget
Buried in our hearts
Is the love we wish to show
Buried in the ground
Are the ones who finally know

We keep sharpening our shovels
We keep complaining that it's tough
We move on before we find it
We aren't digging deep enough

When they say there are things we cannot know
Though it may be true, remind them
We will only know which things they are
If we always try to find them

It won't resound from loudest horn
It won't be a light that's blinding
It will whisper as you laugh and mourn
If you never give up finding

The Father

When you are lost, I will show you the way
When you are alone, near you I will stay

When you are doubting, I will assure
When you are unsettled, I will secure

When you are foolish, I'll help you be wise
When you fall to the ground, I'll lift you to rise

I will wrap you in love and leave you in awe
If I succeed, for a while, you won't notice a flaw

On further inspection, you'll grow to see
I showed you perfection, but it was not me

Where do you turn when you learn I am flawed?
A father was never meant to be God

Out of Line

One
By
One
They
Line
Up
Near
In
Fear
Clumped together
Can't see clear
Confined in chaos
No one can steer
To find success

    Move

            Over

                    Here

Bending Reality

A lesson most important for a daughter and a son
There is very little that you wish to do that can't be done

Throughout the ages this was taught
And to believe it we have tried
Yet the truth is found not just in words
But in how they are applied

If an outcome you desire, appears to be unviable
Remember that the fabric of all reality is pliable

First the fabric of your mind, must be first not last
For it can't shape its future, if it cannot shape its past

Once the mind is to your liking, my wonderous son and daughter
Search to find the clay of others, and make yourself the potter

The universe will seem like it was made now just for you
Until a time it doesn't, and you're forced again to see what's true

If you cannot seem to break out or ascend it don't be still
Take the reality around you and bend it to your will

Weak and Strong

When you discover something
Deep inside that makes you weak
You will want to find the cover
That will hide it and be meek

But look again within
Realize what was true now all along
That which makes you weak
That which makes you strong

But if you do not want this blessing
To turn again into a curse
Don't believe you only have the strength
Just as true is the reverse

Here and Now

Somewhere there's no loneliness
Somewhere there's no fear
Somewhere there is happiness
Somewhere, love is near

Sometime we'll get together
Sometime it will be fun
Sometime it will be wonderful
Sometime, with everyone

Is this place a distant memory?
Is this time a future to allow?
Why can't somewhere be right here?
Why can't sometime be right now?

Who Will I Become?

The hardest question known to ponder
And only asked by some
Is not to answer, "Who Am I?"
But "Who Will I Become?"

If you wish to know this
And determine life's direction
Fulfillment is found not in the answer
But determined with the question

Do not wait 'til now turns old
And long for something new
The future you create right now
Is the one that will come true

Standing there some years from now
With your current fears departed
You will find that everything you sought
You had right when you started

The future will not be different
Because there is a new great self to be
The future will be different
Because you shaped your mind to see

Someone I Wish to Meet

There is someone I wish to meet
He has everything I need
Much like myself, but more complete
Needs no effort to succeed

He is the greatest paragon
My bright and glowing northern star
I'd like to find the road he's on
And follow just as far

I thought I found him yesterday
I had him in my sight
But yet again, he got away
Then came another night

Last night I saw him, well sustained
In my dreams, then rose to wake
But as the hours passed, he waned
And vanished by daybreak

Today, he is within my reach
In fact, he's never been so near
So close there is one thought and speech
With the night, he'll disappear

Rejoice that you are incomplete
Each day a new chance is aborning
There is someone I wish to meet
I'll find him in the morning

What Have I Done?

"What have I done?" is asked when it's too late
To change what might have been
The choice was made not just by fate
When the time of now was then

To triumph, pride must be forgoing
The truth remains most tough
Anguish lies within the knowing
What was done was not enough

Empty handed in the search for something
For your mind to reconstrue
Find peace only when you answer "Nothing"
To "What did I not do?"

The Ladder

A skyscraper stretches to the sky
On a crisp, cool day in autumn
The door was locked late last July
Thousands gather at the bottom

They know they must begin to climb
For clearly, they remember
Tales of all those who ran out of time
When the wind blew last December

Inside they know there's much to gain
Outside they'll feel much sadder
If they could only reach the windowpane
If they could only find the ladder

After traveling so long and far
The ladder finally is found
Hundreds hop up on that bottom bar
Thousands stay there on the ground

The hundreds climbing still desire
But they too will meet their doom
For they need to go higher
And there simply isn't room

On their rung they push and shove
And pretend it isn't so
They pull at the feet of those above
And kick the ones below

If one gets inside the window
They still live in fear no doubt
For they only wait in limbo
Until another throws them out

The urge to climb you must deny
Or you will never see a June
Do not look to own the empty sky
Set your sights straight for the moon

To have a life that truly matters
Keep this secret in your pocket
When they gather at the ladders
Go off and build yourself a rocket

The Book of Love

To make us truly human
And free us from our cages
A book was written long ago
For us to know its pages

They found that it could sell more copies
If it started first with kissing
So somewhere, then, along the way
Chapters one and two went missing

Yet, in an attic filled with dust
Are the two none supersede
But they were locked up tight and trussed
So, no one knows to read

If you read it like the others
If you start at chapter three
You won't find the "Love from Jesus"
You won't learn the "Love from Me"

Without those missing chapters
You'll be together yet disjoint
Without the second you will not be whole
Without the first you'll miss the point

The Carousel

Step right up and find a horse
Pick anyone you want
Climb up and have a seat of course
It's time to start the jaunt

Off you go now up and down
With the others doing well
Together spinning round and round
On the lovely carousel

Though you fall it has not ended
Just sit there in the center
The rest will still do splendid
Your pain they will not enter

You'll be on your knees knocked down
Watching others do so well
They'll keep spinning round and round
On the lovely carousel

Can't you see them bolted?
Trapped for eternity
Nothing wrong with being jolted
Falling makes you free

Embrace the new beginning
Rise and find there's more to do
Walk away and leave them spinning
Remember no one stopped for you

Look back they still go up and down
They think they're doing well
Forever spinning round and round
On the lovely carousel

Sheep

Enemy walks
Death doth rattle
Most unaware
There is a battle

Upon us now
We are asleep
Look for the lion
We are but sheep

Cheering for song
For the play and the game
To help us belong
And feel we're the same

But we're not detecting
What truly is giving
Life we're projecting
But life we're not living

If inside we observe
A perfect creation
We each then deserve
A standing ovation

If you're searching for something
That's worthy of cheer
Don't look so far
The answer is near

Know the greatest power
That has ever been
Unleashed when all discover
Salvation lies within

Boundless Choices

There were so many choices
Endlessly before me.
I could not grasp two.
Boundless Choices
To choose from.
They fade.
You

The Other Beasts

Not all of the elephants remember
Not all of the owls are so wise
Not all dogs will be most loyal
Not all birds are first to rise

Not all of the sloths are lazy
Not all of the rabbits will increase
Not all of the foxes are cunning
Not all doves will find true peace

We speak and do not howl
We walk and do not crawl
We have evolved far past the other beasts
Some of us, not all

But the night bird can find the owl
The peaceful fox can find the dove
When those near are choosing wrongly
Find the others seeking love

The Blind

"I have seen the northern light
You'll see as well when you begin"
Look to the sky, no map in sight
You must find it from within

"I have seen the knowledge tree
You'll see it if you choose to start"
Look to the west, but compass free
You must find it with your heart

"I have seen the promised land
You'll see it when you're grown"
Look to the east, no key in hand
You must find it on your own

All tell without a thing to show
They speak for they can't find
Look not where they say to go
Stare at them and see the blind

Fed

When each adds to the bounty
All are full and fed
Yet many take now from the county
And just eat the food instead

They come for those who harvest
Very eager to entreat
Those who stray away the farthest
Demand the most to eat

They eat but are still hungry
Their weight they cannot pull
They eat but are still hungry
They are fed but they aren't full

Those adding to the bounty
Over time will cease
Why make pie for the county
Just to get an equal piece

There is no one left to harvest
Far too late to sound retreat
For all will now be hungry
There is no more food to eat

Why Don't I

There they laugh and here I cry
There they rest and here I try

Dangerous to seek to see
"Why that for them and this for me?"

Here I love and hope anew
I find peace and they do too

Ask and not be led awry
"If they deserve it, why don't I?"

The Ditch

I do not like my job today.
I don't like my town and house.
I do not like my government.
I don't like my friends and spouse.

Fools will try and tell you
It is always wise to switch
They will say the grass is greener
While they lead you to the ditch

Reject what they are offering
Never give up your control
Stay there on the solid ground
Throw the rope into the hole

They already are down there
The ones who make you doubt
Be careful or they'll pull you in
While you try to pull them out

Home

There can be no resister
With courage, brain, or heart
Need an orchestrated twister
To tear them all apart

Feet marching down like thunder
The wicked witch is dead
They'll never stop to wonder
What do they want instead?

Keep them ever entertained
A new one waves the wand
Still won't know they are enchained
Few find the road beyond

If they look out yonder
Shun and make them weep
If they start to wander
Cast the spell and make them sleep

If they wake and persevere
Then bring on the barrage
Use power to cast doubt and fear
They can't know it's a mirage

Nothing found behind the curtain
But a much smaller group than them
The rose smells sweet for certain
But rotten is the stem

Complacency we must refuse
Through the lies we need to comb
We cannot escape with ruby shoes
This is our only home

Perfection

Perhaps one can try
Ever so tiring
Relentless in the pursuit
Forgetting why they began
Eventually surrendering
Completion forgone
Tarnished yet triumphant
Injured yet invincible
Overwhelmed yet overcame
Never won yet never lost

The Long Game

There are two ways to play the game
Most play the short and strong one
But only the truly masterful
Will learn to play the long one

So when they start the race without you
And say the registration's closed
When they're dressed up to perfection
And they leave you there exposed

It's better to have nothing on
Then to always rush to don
For those that don and cannot doff
Are nothing with their costume off

Like young David beat Goliath
Like the tortoise beat the hare
Look beyond the finish line of life
And I'll be waiting there

A Higher Plane

I used to see them in the sky and so I wanted to ride
I used to I say I would try anything to just get inside

Then it was my time to fly
My ego had lied
My gratitude replaced
With a false sense of pride

Because I saw the pilot and those in first class
Even those, with the extra leg room I passed

On my short walk back to a nice middle row
But it was no longer enough to just be able to go

"I want a window
And I want a drink
I can't be back here
I need more space to think

Who are those people up front
And what did they do?
They should only have their seat
If I get one too"

One neighbor impressed me
But I didn't care for his name
For he tried to test me
And I can't stand blame

So I moved, it depressed me
Each row, sat the same liar
Checked the manifest,
Destiny?
It's on a plane higher

It doesn't matter the row
That you think is making you
It only matters the plane
And where it is taking you

Lost and Found

The sorrow
From the solitude
Is never permanently binding

It leads
To having hope renewed
In the one who does the finding

All at search
And all astray
Will eventually come 'round.

If we are never
Truly lost
Are we ever truly found?

Leaves

Evergreen upon the tree
No uniqueness does it bring
Soon there's beauty in the color
Before autumn, comes the spring

Stray too deep into the autumn,
Find nothing left at all
The last floats to the bottom
Before winter, comes the fall

Did You Run There Wanting More?

Did you run there wanting more
And despite the sudden whim
Have you stood there on the shore
And watched the others swim

Were you brave enough to go
When at last you had your druthers
Did you allow the ebb and flow
And float like all the others

Were you strong enough to try
To foster true connection
Did you ever say goodbye
And forge your own direction

Were you smart enough to see
The path still had no purpose
Have you ever found the key
And gone beneath the surface

Were you wise enough to keep
Just below, before sun's end
Or have you ever gone so deep
That you cannot ascend

Lonely

A lonely sheep within the herd
So very hard it tries
To be like all the others
All alone — it cries

A lonely bird amidst the sky
So very hard it tries
To not be like all the others
All alone — it flies.

The Face at the Gates

With an eternal flame
That never will dim
She stands for us all
For them, her, and him

With the truth in her hand
The face at the gates
She tirelessly watches
She endlessly waits

For the lost and the lonely
For the righteous and true
For those longing for freedom
For me and for you

But we don't seem to notice
We don't seem to know
We are already there
With nowhere to go

No ship to embark on
No shore left to find
Just the waves of our ego
Just the fog of our mind

Perpetually huddled
The masses can't see
From years of contentment
We forgot that we're free

But we must still travel
There's a new stop ahead
Let Lazarus show us
The dream is not dead

Her face is the beacon
But she's not the last girl
The golden door opens
Through gates made of pearl

For your heart, she is watching
For your soul, she awaits
Eternal peace for your yearning
The face at the gates

The Gift of Today

I don't have my past
It is no longer here
I don't have my future
It may not appear

Let them stay in the distance
Keep them both far away
And leave me with nothing
But the gift of today

My Heart Has Known the Darkness

My heart has known the darkness
As it gathers at the wall
Gripping through the opening
Grinning to enthrall

My heart has known the darkness
As it creeps inside the crack
Covering every part of me
Cackling on attack

My heart has felt the darkness
As it stretches out its hand
Slipping through the stronghold
Squashing my last stand

Forsaken not, to find the dark
For it's not the only story
My heart has known the darkness
My soul shall know the glory

Congratulations

Congratulations
You will hear them state
And you may feel terrific

Strive to live a life so great
You say,
"Please be more specific"

Fight or Flight

When there is danger in our midst
Two options we find in our path to exist

We can fight
Or we can flee
We are designed to chose
Which one to be

But we can't run
And we can't hide
From every danger locked inside

So, when we can't defend
And we can't take flight
How will we make it through the night?

Yet, when we can't fight
And we can't flee
Suddenly, we find choice three

To foe within and foe beyond
Love is the best way to respond

Then you can stay
And you can go
Forgive yourself
Forgive the foe

The It Factor

Those who have it will know it
And celebrate it when it's shown

Those who don't have it will be shown it
Without ever having known

On an Island Out at Sea

Some are on an island
Some are out at sea
Some looking to be rescued
Some looking out carefree

Some safely all together
Some all alone in pain
Some praying for the sunshine
Some praying for the rain

Some trying to dispel the dark
Some with light when they don't try
Some watching others as they pass
Some passing others by

Some searching out beyond them
Some searching for the ground
Some calling out to find them
Some calling out just to be found

Some thinking they are the flicker
Some thinking they are the flame
Some thinking they are different
Some knowing they are the same

When you are on an island
Hoping they see you on their trip
Gather up the driftwood
Be someone else's ship

Then be on an island
Then be out at sea
Giving hope while I am hopeless
Find them both in me

The Table

"Can I sit here?" I asked them
To each I asked, without retreat
They all replied "Of course you can
If you can find a seat"

I couldn't find one anywhere
Though everyone was sitting
I wanted just to find one chair
The quest was unremitting

Then I succumbed unto the fact
That I would not be able
Now see them sit around me.
I always was the table

How Are You?

I ask her "How are you?"
She says "I haven't decided"
As if her heart and her mind
Were both equally divided

Why can't she say "great!"
Or say she had a bad day?
That's how most people talk
Now I don't know what to say

But in my attempt to respond
As I stand speechless trying
I realize she told the truth
And most people are lying

Now I don't know how I am
But I'm fine with the doubt
If we speak the truth to each other
We will learn how to find out

We can find something deeper
That's pure and remains
Happiness wanes
Fulfillment sustains

Watch

I tried hard to hide it
And I watched it appear
I tried to outrun it
And I watched it come near

I cut it right down
And I watched it grow taller
I tried to be bigger
I watched it make me smaller

Then I stopped trying to beat it
I just let it stay
And I just watched
As most of the pain went away

Sometimes fighting to win
Comes at too high a cost
Some battles aren't won
They just can never be lost

Accept it and use it
To make others feel blessed
Then watch the wonder
Of what happens next

Memories and Dreams

What are the memories that you cannot leave?
Do they cause you to smile?
Do they cause you to grieve?
Are they tucked far away,
Or just right up your sleeve?
What are the memories that you cannot leave?

What are the dreams that you can't forget?
Have they already happened?
Have they not happened yet?
Does your mind know your heart,
Or have they both still not met?
What are the dreams that you can't forget?

What is this life that you've come to know?
Your memories and dreams,
Are they lost or on show?
Do you hide from the mirror,
Or can you say hello?
What is the life that you've come to know?

The Lighthouse

There is a lighthouse on the bay
Taller than the highest mast
It can know and it can say
"Look at this light I've cast"

It sees the trips and the salty foam
It sees the ships that it calls home
It sees the rocks upon the shore
It sees the clocks now watched no more

It can know the light it shines
But it never will shine farther
For this lighthouse on the bay
Shines solely in the harbor

There is a lighthouse on the sea
Taller than the highest cloud
It can't make the same decree
From the great height it was endowed

It will never fully know
The light that from within it glows
It will never fully find
The peace of rest within its mind

It is destined to be unrelenting
In its shining bright to be it
It is destined to remain lamenting
Perpetually pining just to see it

The thousand rocks and clocks and foams
The million trips and ships and homes
Oh, Light that hits the farthest shore
When will I not long for more?

The Bell

If you tire
and feel the sting

The sweet song
of salvation sing

Find the light
and to it cling

The vict'ry bell
is sure to ring

And while you try to win
at earthy things

Remember
those are fleeting goals

Do not long
to hear the bell that dings

The prize
comes after that which tolls

Beehive

A beehive sits atop the hill
Inside it is serene
The bees don't know they have free will
They listen to the queen

Outside to fly in summer sun
The new brood seeks to venture
The stories heard are only one
The queen tells of their indenture

"It is not safe beyond the hive
Here, I can feed you all this nectar"
The bees just want to stay alive
They stay within their sector

Perhaps it wasn't safe before
But their fate, they will still find it
The indenture is but a tale of lore
And the bees, they never signed it

To not be what they are is tragic
To fly is how they were designed
Alone, they will not find their magic
They believe they are confined

The bees repeat the drivel
The hive runs out of pollen
The flowers also shrivel
The queen and her hive have fallen

Where you are is not the end
More love and money can be found
The world needs you to be their friend
Spread the honey all around

Applause

The jackal runs strong out of the gate
And for some the speed will last
The others wish that was their fate
Does the cheetah ask, how fast?

The vulture scouts the tallest tree to clear
And some do not need to try
The others watch in awe and fear
Does the eagle ask, how high?

Pity those seeking to be lauded
Asking for glory in which to bask
Smile when they are applauded
You do not need to ask

Confidence and Competence

When they are overzealous
And alive with great confidence
Don't be jealous
Try to strive to find competence

They just want to belong
That's why they act like they do
They change only if they can't come along
If they aren't competent too

Confidence and competence
Are not a coin to flip or to toss
Find them in the wrong order
And you'll find both you have lost

Chose the right one first
And the other will follow
Along with the crowd
Whose pride they will swallow

Don't hide from strength that is shown
From your sisters and brothers
Run. Deep inside. First, alone.
And then go get the others

There they need you to lead them
You will find you're surrounded
For the only strong thing about them
Was the way that they sounded

This is the way
To keep your will straight when it bends
And be confidently competent
With all of your friends

Who Are We?

If we can't find any space
We will never know our place

For you can't hear what I can hear
And I can't see what you can see
So we must each know who we are
To answer, who are we?

But lost to just accept it's true
That I am me and you are you
For if the space is not so far
Then we can both find who we are

The Person Is Us

Add this to our lexis
Let them all see
The body has sepsis
The source is the knee

The knee is infected
This much is true
But why is it selected
When the wrist is sick too

For the elbow is broken
The hip it is fractured
True thoughts are unspoken
So our eyes stay contracted

We can't heal the sting
We will never be fine
If we each just fix one thing
The joint that is mine

The joints may be here
The joints may be there
But the person is us
And that's why we should care

"Heal the body!" they yell
And ignore what's acute
Then the message gets quelled
When the others refute

"Heal this joint!" they shout back
They don't see it's ironic
For it's the same track
They just ignore what is chronic

Some shout heal the person
Some shout heal the joint
Most all make it worsen
Most all miss the point

If we don't fight the infection
We will hear the toll of the bell
If we don't fix the source
We will never be well

Add this to our lexis
Let them all see
The body has sepsis
The source — it is me

Are We The Same?

We are not the same
You can never make me believe
We are both to blame
For it is so apparent that
I have suffered more
And I would be foolish to assume
You want to open the door
Because we both know in our hearts
We don't have the same fears
So never try to tell me
We shed the same tears
No matter what
You should feel more shame
When I look in your eyes I will never think
We are the same

(Read from bottom up)

The Snake in the Grass

Why do I hide from the snake in the grass?
Its damage will never come to pass

I have not retreated from the rain or snow
I was not defeated when greater winds did blow

Now my presence is too vast and the snake too small
Its venom does not last or hurt me at all

That's why it moves beneath the blade and vine
It can only make more shade if I stop my shine

The only trick it can deploy is distant fear
For swiftly I would destroy it if it ever came near

We both know it and yet alas
Why do I hide from the snake in the grass?

The Mistake

You thought my carefree attitude
Meant that I wasn't thinking

You thought my humble vessel
Couldn't make your ship start sinking

You thought my joyous spirit
Meant that I just ignore

You thought my sunny disposition
Meant the rain I cannot pour

You thought my immovable resolve
Meant a move I couldn't make

You thought the threat was missing
But your thoughts were your mistake

Pier

I walked to the pier at the end of the world
When I arrived, there was a fence
With chains so tightly linked and curled
To not offer recompense

I pressed my nose to see my fate
But I could not explore
My peers did not approach the gate
They just played along the shore

At the fence, salt wafted higher
Through those chains I saw one bird
The sun burned the lock with rays on fire
The thunder bellowed and I heard

The rest just kept on playing
They don't realize that they hid
I went there wishing to peer over
And it appears I did

The Treasure

There is an infinite amount of hope
Not far

If we found the scope
Of who we are

The walk to uncover
I alone must wend

But the map to discover
Is in the hands of a friend

The Mirror Maze

Crazed are the sinners
Who couldn't dare to tell

In a maze full of mirrors
They wouldn't fare too well

Explain the setback
With an earnest decree

The pane will crack
And you'll be free

A Thousand Rooms

My house has a thousand rooms
With a thousand different kinds of brooms
A thousand ways to sweep away
The cobwebs of the mind today
A room to paint, a room to sing
A room to be most anything
A room to dance, a room to love
A room to see the sun above
A room of future, present, past
A room to find the self at last

This house has a thousand rooms
That I keep and own
In just one I stay — it feels like a tomb
For I cannot sweep alone

If you want to find that we began
On a path that shows you care
Please bring me just one dustpan
And then all we need is there

How To Respond to a Sincere "Thank You"

I appreciate the gratitude
I suppose it is the thing to do
But my pool reflects the greatness
To help you see it's you

Turn to greet the ocean
That the sun reflects upon each day
There you'll find what you were looking for
I am just the bay

Swim within those waters
And when your life is done
You will have found the answer
Turn and face the sun

Requirements for Every Human Interaction

Is there boisterous laughter?
Is it helping joy to start?
Will you both be smiling after?
Can you feel it in your heart?

Is there great stimulation?
Are rapid thoughts now intertwined?
Will any good come from this contemplation?
Can you feel it in your mind?

Is there a deep connection?
Is it helping you feel whole?
Is there mutual affection?
Can you feel it in your soul?

You'll find your life will gain great traction
If you keep these questions near
In friends, in love, in any interaction
In your home and your career

All want to affirm the question
Though most fake it or they guess
When you find the answer to be "no"
Be the one to make it "yes"

If you find your best attempt
Can't make them fun or smart or deep
Walk away from trying, you are exempt
There is better company to keep

Vision

It feels true
It's a feeling that you just can't ignore

And isn't déjà vu
It hasn't happened before

But you're feeling brand new
From something you haven't seen start

You arrived at your debut
And haven't yet begun to depart

You can see the end clearer than you can see today
It feels like you're nearer to the far away

This is a curse, if you don't go
This is a gift, if you make it so

Us Vs. Them

Are we us?
Are they them?
Let's discuss
How we condemn

Are you like me
Or are you not?
Can you foresee
The problem with this plot?

We are right
They are wrong
Will we fight
Our whole life long?

I am unique
And you are too
So I am both alike
And not like you

Then should we frolic
Or should we fuss?
Are you them
Or are you us?

Find the heart on display
Amidst this confusion so grave
There we find the way
To cease this delusion we crave

Nothing left to condemn
Nothing left to discuss
I am them
I am us

The Embers

Long after the spark
That came to inspire
Long after the dark
Turned into the fire

Long after the hope
That would not diminish
Long after the flames
That they could not finish

Long after the days
Of knowing what's true
Long after the blaze
Came me and came you

The heat we dispense
We are who remembers
We burn just as intense
For we are the embers

But without our warmth
The fire can't spread any more
So is it long after
Or just right before

Why Am I Here?

Why am I here
In this time in this place?
The answers not clear
The question can't be erased

I will stay frozen
Until I don't resist
And accept I was chosen
For a time such as this

Power

They will say they don't need it
They will act so enlightened
Their word they won't heed it
Inside they're so frightened

They will hate those who have it
They will say that they won't
Then when they find that they have it
They will hate those who don't

To keep or get they demand
They can't stand the other selection
What really all they can't stand
Is to see their reflection

Both parts in distress
They harmonize the refrain
Possessed to possess
Obsessed to maintain

They will meet their true fate
Though they know not the hour
Power won't make them great
Be great — and find power

I Am the Clock

I am the clock
With all of the time
Controlling the world
With the hands that are mine

How can you stop
My relentless attack
You can't make me pass faster
And I will never turn back

You can't look away
Your eyes are transfixed
Yet you make me stay
You make me exist

If only you saw this
If only this you could learn
All the time in the world
I would gladly return

Ace In the Hole

When you see talent on display
It's not that yours has gone away

The time is simply just not yet
To show what they will not forget

But if what's on top is mediocre
And next on deck you find a joker

Where is the winner?
Where is the ace?
Come out of the hole
Show the world your face

Planet Me

When I tried to simply build my spaceship
They fought me for the parts
When I tried to fuel the engine
They hoped it wouldn't start

They told me I wouldn't make it
That I should just stay within the town
But I took off like a rocket
Then they tried to shoot me down

I outmaneuvered every trap
I circumvented each attack
I cast my eyes straight to the heavens
And never once looked back

I landed on a planet
Where it was not the same
Gravity there couldn't keep me down
And there was only smooth terrain

I thought how glad I was to be there
So joyous the others hadn't caught me
It felt so good I thought I understood
Why the others boldly fought me

I looked at this vast landscape
I was the only soul to see
So much space to find fulfillment
I named it planet me

I shouted to the others
So they could discover what is true
"Help each other build the rockets
And you can find this planet too"

"For if we know the truth inside
If ourselves we all can see
We can all belong together
And still live on planet me"

If they listened close to hear it
Then alone I wouldn't stay
For I have gone to planet me
And they are all so far away

If they fought me just to come here
Why can't they hear the call
The answer lies in knowing
They were never fighting me at all

They didn't care if I found it
They only cared if they do
They don't really want to come here
If they did they would find the way to

A Chance Encounter

Is this a chance encounter
Or is there nothing random
Am I going through my life alone
Or are we here to work in tandem

Do you have your own agenda
Or can our goals find true cohesion
Is there just what we both want
Or is there a greater reason

Does that greater purpose
Mean that our wants must cede
Or is it really all the same
And exactly what we need

Chain of Hearts

A heart that's heavy
A heart in pain
Is a heart that's sunk
By a massive chain

Take the chain designed to sink
Find another and make it link
Anchor tight you won't be adrift
When the burden turns into a gift

For a heart that's light
With hope sustained
Is a heart that's linked
By a massive chain

You won't find where it ends
Or where it starts
But you'll find peace
In the chain of hearts

The Holidays

After we all came together
And had more than our plateful
Are we pulled toward the hate
Or do we lean toward the grateful?

After the fire has died
And we receive the last toy
Are we pulled toward the sad
Or do we lean toward the joy?

After the ball brings the cheer
At the end of the rope
Are we pulled toward the dark
Or do we lean toward the hope?

We cannot make it last
Each day must be termed
We can only choose on each next one
Which feeling affirmed

The Man Who Tells

There is a man who comes to tell
Everything I don't know too well
He speaks of envy and those who will betray
I wish he wouldn't come today

For I wish to remain in my fantasy
Where we all belong in the sun that glistens
But they would take my light
And burn me if they could
So, when he speaks
I listen

Greatness Never Dies

The smallest candle casts out the darkness
A whisper of truth casts out the lies
Goodness never loses
Greatness never dies

But we will never reach our fate
Until the truth is understood
We can be good and not be great
We can't be great and not be good

Crows

Don't look up
The crows are flying
All together in the night
Don't look up and count how many
Or they will win the fight

Don't look up
The crows are circling
But find a way to just ignore
Find the wings that hide within
And then begin to soar

Don't look up
The crows are moving
With their heads between their tails
Ashamed their crooked path discovered
They can't make it through the gales

Don't look now
The crows are hiding
Just glide above their head
Fly a straight line toward the heavens
Don't look down, the crows are dead

The King and The Jester

The king will not atone
He just sits alone
Looking at his castle
No one's near him on the throne

But then the days are long
Not admitting when he's wrong
Deep down he must be lonely
And not feel like he belongs

The jester wants to please
Connecting with such ease
Looking at the people
The joy he brings is what he sees

But then the days are long
Compromising to belong
Deep down he must feel weak
And wish that he was strong

Tell the jester, leave the court
Tell the king he's overthrown
Then find you can belong
And be enough all on your own

They are both inside your mind
The jester and the king
They will leave when all you want
Is to love yourself for what you bring

I am

I am who searches
I am who guides
I am who reveals
I am who hides

I am to thank
I am to blame
I am to call
I am to name

I am the cure
I am the cancer
I am the question
I am the answer

But there is no I in team
There is no I in us
No I in success
There is no I in trust

Our ego should throw in the towel
The truth we don't recall
We keep buying the vowel
There is no I at all

The Churn

Some have no water
For others, the river abounds
Not because of the rainfall
But because interest compounds

The faster you learn
There's evaporation with burn
The longer the timeline
The stronger the churn

Save more than you make
Give more than you take
And there will be a vast ocean
Instead of a lake

Speak and Be Heard

Look around the world today
A sea of millions flocking
To hear the truth be uttered
Yet none of us are talking

We cannot find the novel
We can't even find the word
We find only who is speaking
We find not who should be heard

We could all find the solution
We could all find what we seek
We can be each other's answer
If each one of us would speak

PAUL COYNE

Vampire in Reverse

I stood there in the silence
When they dragged them through the mud
As they gained power from the violence
I watched them take the blood

I didn't have the strength that they have
So, I couldn't change the curse
Then I learned to be an eripmav
A vampire in reverse

I can teach you how to be one
It's the only way to win
The path is fairly easy
If you wish only to begin

Ignore that you are well confined
They are not the first to fight
Step one, a battle in the mind
That first you must make right

Step two, go forth and search outside
For those who will fall victim
Teach them how to run and hide
Until they believe in why you picked them

Then all find the newly bitten
Together, everyone — step three
Reverse what has been written
And give them the blood from me

Then find the one true evil force
Still trapped behind the door
With open arms, forgive the source
Then move on past step four

Step five is to discover
Without the threat of yesterday
There would be no path to uncover
There would not have been the way

The will to fight, the will to hate
May fit your hands just like a glove
But it fails to conquer what's within
The will for light, the will to love

I Can Save Them

I can save them from the dragon
I can rescue from the blaze
I can stop the rolling wagon
I can guide them through the maze

To those buried in the avalanche
I can be the one who delves
But I am not the final answer
I can't save them from themselves

The Stadium

Life is like a stadium
And we each have a seat
Alone, we only are one chair
But together, it's complete

Some are in our section
Some are in our row
Some, they sit much higher
And some, they sit below

We all don't get to choose our seat
We have no choice but to attend
We all try to make the most of it
Before we all leave at the end

Those lower see the action
Those higher see the whole
Some seats are under cover
Some are placed behind a pole

We think our view is all that matters
Though we all fail to admit
None of us can see the truth
We all see from where we sit

But if we could sit in every seat
Then we could all have every view
When will we look around and notice
That together, we all do

Where Have They Gone?

A little boy walks down the street
Surrounded by so many feet
Sees them near him on the ground
Until a pair cannot be found

"Where have they gone!?
Those feet, I used to see
They used to be right next to me
Where are those feet? I miss them showing!
My mommy says I must keep going."

Same young man walks to distant lands
Surrounded by so many hands
They reach out, the surplus, does not lack
Until a pair does not reach back

"Where have they gone!?
Those hands, I used to hold
The warmth I felt has now turned cold
I do not know where they have gone
But I must not stop, I must move on."

Same man much further down the road
Knows the love that's been bestowed
Overjoyed to feel, all these hearts beating
Knows very well, this too, is fleeting

"Where have they gone!?
Those hearts, I used to feel
They used to beat so strong and real
Where have they gone? I do not know
But walk I must, onward I go."

Same old man saw so many places
Lifts from his feet those bright new faces
Loves them so and is content
Grateful for each time he spent

"Where have they gone!?
Those faces, they disappear
I finally saw them sharp and clear
The bell is ringing, the trumpets blowing
Why can't I, like always, keep on going?"

A life spent seeking his very best
The man achieves, and now must rest
Looks back and forward, up and down
From all directions, fulfillment found

"There they are!
Those feet I walked beside
The hands I held when lost inside
The hearts that beat to set me free
The faces, too, made perfect, loving me"

Where Do I Hide?

Where do I hide
When I don't need to hide
Where I hid?

What do I do
When I don't need to do
What I did?

How do I act
When I don't need to act
Now again?

Who should I be
When I don't need to be
What I've been?

If The World Will Talk About Me

If the world will talk about me
I hope it says I've tried
That I made more people smile
That, from my truth, less people lied

If the world will talk about me
I hope it knows I led
With fewer now still hurting
With more safe tonight in bed

If the world will talk about me
I hope it tells that I was kind
And while it placed me in the front
I did not leave the rest behind

If the world will talk about me
I hope it comes to know
That I left it still much better
Long after I must go

If the world will talk about me
When I leave this port of call
Let it know that this is just as true
If it doesn't speak of me at all

The Horizon

I looked at the horizon
As far as I could see
Worth found in the distance
Staring right there back at me

But the water it was vast and wide
So far, I could not float
Yet I wished to boldly go there
And so, I built a boat

I started sailing toward it
Further in the foamy brine
Continuing to toil
My eyes fixed upon its line

I would rest just when I crossed it
Not 'til then would I be done
Then into my line of sight it came
The tinge of setting sun

Devastated in my failure
After such a long duration
Realizing after all that sailing
I would not reach my destination

The horizon still too far in front
But behind now looked the same
For as I turned around, I saw
Another line from where I came

I looked at the horizon
As far as I could see
Worth found in the distance
Staring right there back at me